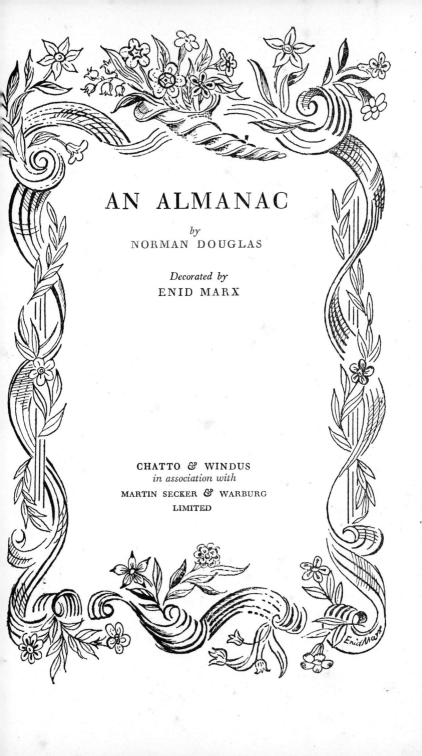

AN ALMANAC

by
NORMAN DOUGLAS

Decorated by
ENID MARX

CHATTO & WINDUS
in association with
MARTIN SECKER & WARBURG
LIMITED

PUBLISHED BY
Chatto & Windus, London
in association with
Martin Secker & Warburg Ltd., London
*
Oxford University Press, Toronto

1945
PRINTED IN GREAT BRITAIN

NOTE

As a "small return for great kindness" I manu-
factured this ALMANAC out of extracts from such
of my books as were on the spot (most of them
were). The Livraria Portugália of Lisbon in 1941
printed twenty-five copies, all but one being given
to friends. These seemed to like the venture. If
that be so, then others may not dislike it either.
Hence this edition, which contains a few alterations.

The opinions expressed are not necessarily my
own, nor need they be taken too seriously. Just
a little diversion. . . .

N. D.

For

VIVA AND WILLIE KING

JANUARY

· 1 ·

The business of life is to enjoy oneself; everything else is a mockery.

· 2 ·

The whole earth reeks of humanity and its works. One has to be old and tough to appraise them at their true worth.

· 3 ·

Where words cease, music begins. Where music ceases, kissing begins.

· 4 ·

No authentic child of man will fit into a novel. History is the place for such people; history, or oblivion.

· *5* ·

The antagonism of flesh and spirit, the most pernicious piece of crooked thinking which has ever oozed out of our deluded brain.

· *6* ·

A sound schooling should have a dual aim—to equip a man for hours of work and for hours of leisure. They interact; if the leisure is misspent, the work will suffer.

· *7* ·

Is there no prosperity other than commercial? It is surely time to have done with this utilitarian nonsense.

· *8* ·

I should be interested to discover what proportion of unsatisfactory marriages is due to the bare fact that the male partner does not know his business.

· *9* ·

Abuse, hearty abuse, is a tonic to all save men of indifferent health.

· *10* ·

Elaborate urns, sarcophagi of carven alabaster, are cajoleries which flatter the survivors and yield poor comfort to those who lie within.

· *11* ·

One owes something to oneself: *n'est-ce pas?*

· *12* ·

Life, once the gift of a jealous god, has become a mere series of readjustments, and "nature" the summary of our experience of them.

· *13* ·

Humour is essentially a product of ease, and nobody can be at ease in unquiet times.

· *14* ·

The standardization of youth proceeds relentlessly. It is one of many steps in the direction of that termite-ideal towards which we are trending.

· *15* ·

I have been perusing Seneca's letters. He was
a cocoa-drinker, masquerading as an ancient.

· *16* ·

To save himself the trouble of inventing any
fresh shapes, he created them in his own image.

· *17* ·

It is one of the maladies of our age to profess a
frenzied allegiance to truth in unimportant matters,
to refuse consistently to face her where graver
issues are at stake.

· *18* ·

Novelty is of an aphrodisiacal nature, fruit
untasted being ever the best, and better stolen
than bought.

· *19* ·

The ideal cuisine should display an individual
character; it should offer a menu judiciously chosen
from the kitchen-workshops of the most diverse
lands and peoples—a menu reflecting the master's
alert and fastidious taste.

· 20 ·

There is such a thing as a noble resignation; to defy fate, even if one cannot rule it. Many of us northerners would be the better for a little *mektoub*.

· 21 ·

Old Stella, who polished off her thousandth lover not long ago, has just bought a fresh nose. She mislaid her last, and the first one ran away.

· 22 ·

Who will deny that forests, once they have abandoned their hostile attitude to man's progress upon earth, exercise a benignant power, subtle and profound, upon the mind of a people?

· 23 ·

There are enthusiasts who clamour for an international language. International common sense would be more to the point.

· 24 ·

Despotism, priestcraft, and proletariat have ever been good friends; a kind of freemasonry, unintelligible to simple folk, has conjoined them from time immemorial.

· 25 ·

I pick up an average novel now and then, and ask myself whether we shall go on reading this flatulent balderdash much longer.

· 26 ·

Everything becomes legend, if the gentleman will have the goodness to wait.

· 27 ·

Diligent experimentation has taught me to believe that coca will transport you into a Paradise where Venus may be seen, but not touched.

· 28 ·

An old Hebrew, who taught the pleasures of a virtuous life after exhausting those of a voluptuous one, said: Go to the ant. He forgot to remember that the ant sleeps for half the year.

· 29 ·

The next best thing to leading others astray is to be led astray oneself.

· *30* ·

Why amass with dear money the masterpieces of art, when a friendly word will purchase those of nature?

· *31* ·

An English word is no fossil to be locked up in a cabinet, but a living thing, liable to the fate of all such things. Glance back into Chaucer and note how they have thriven on their own merits . . . thriven, or perished, or put on new faces.

FEBRUARY

· 1 ·

Mechanics, not microbes, are the menace to civilization.

· 2 ·

Solitude has a refining and tonic influence; there we wrestle with our thoughts and set them in order; there we nurture the imagination and sow the seeds of character.

· 3 ·

Suffering is ugly; it was reserved for Christianity—Orientalism, I should say—to discover its macabre fascination.

· 4 ·

The world of thought has not expanded; it has contracted and grown provincial.

· 5 ·

We discourse like sages and drink like swine.
Peace with Honour . . .

· 6 ·

The ever-alert, the conscientiously wakeful—
how many fine things they fail to see!

· 7 ·

Reviewers should have a fair dose of personal
worldly experience.   This is what they often lack,
and it accounts for a certain thinness, a certain
anaemic quality, in their appraisals.

· 8 ·

Has any man ever attained to inner harmony
by pondering the experience of others?

· 9 ·

Why prolong life save to prolong pleasure?

· *10* ·

All folklore is saturated with lust of gold and earthly possessions, like the talk of common people in every part of the world.

· *11* ·

They who are all things to their neighbours cease to be anything to themselves.

· *12* ·

It is with publishers as with wives: one always wants somebody else's. And when you have them, where's the difference?

· *13* ·

"But" is the most misused and debilitating monosyllable in the English language. And "very" is my aversion.

· *14* ·

The existence of a Grand Inquisitor is not so much to the discredit of Roman Catholicism as of that delectable spirit which is liable to be generated by any and every kind of faith in a jealous God.

· *15* ·

Every man is a solitary in his griefs. One soon finds that out.

· *16* ·

It takes a wise man to handle a lie. A fool had better remain honest.

· *17* ·

"Never stop working," he once told me. An awful doctrine.

· *18* ·

Delve into the living world and strive to bind yourself to its movement by a chain of your own welding.

· *19* ·

Is not the whole trend of our legislation a sustained effort to pamper the unfit at the expense of the fit?

11

· 20 ·

A man's worst enemy is his own empty stomach.

· 21 ·

Honest men are sometimes hard to please. I have met two or three.

· 22 ·

A plague has infected the world—the plague of repression.

· 23 ·

We cannot lay claim to a truthful state of mind. In this respect the eighteenth century, for all its foppery, was ahead of ours.

· 24 ·

I like to taste my friends but not to eat them; in other words, I hold the old-fashioned view that all interrogation, all social curiosity, is vulgar.

· *25* ·

Travel-books and everything else grow stale; they lose their bloom and freshness. It is we who lose it. The desire to learn is abated, atrophied.

· *26* ·

Fear not, O Mortal, the bark of a certain wrathful Lamb. It is worse than his bite.

· *27* ·

Your good man sticks at nothing. He is a jest on the part of the gods; their only jest, and a poor one.

· *28* ·

The heroes, the saints and sages—they are those who face the world alone.

· *29* ·

Poverty is like rain. It drops down ceaselessly, disintegrating the finer tissues of a man, his recent, delicate adjustments, and leaving nothing but the bleak and gaunt framework. A poor man is a wintry tree, alive, but stripped of its shining splendour.

MARCH

· 1 ·

Be quick to love, and slow to die.

· 2 ·

Our disrespect for the human frame is another relic of monasticism. In fact our whole education is tainted with the monkish spirit.

· 3 ·

Your Anglo-Saxon is always worth listening to when he talks about cruel sports.

· 4 ·

There is a kinship, a kind of freemasonry, between all persons of intelligence, however antagonistic their moral outlook.

· *5* ·

These mortals have no sense of fun. Their very laughter smells of death.

· *6* ·

That venerable blunder: to think that in changing the form of government you change the heart of man.

· *7* ·

Be sober; let the loved one drink.

· *8* ·

Year by year our hard-won domestic privileges have been gnawed or lopped away. The recent history of the English citizen is one long wail of liberties forfeited.

· *9* ·

When people cease to reflect, they become idealists.

15

· 10 ·

Excess of sentiment, like all other intemperance, is the mark of that unsober and unsteady beast—the crowd.

· 11 ·

Uphill work, trying to shock an old lady of today!

· 12 ·

They argued, and never ceased arguing, about the welfare of their spirit—as though it were something quite apart from the welfare of their body.

· 13 ·

Know thyself: to what depths of vain, egocentric brooding has that dictum led!

· 14 ·

We create a word for our convenience and forthwith, unless we are on the look-out, there comes over it a horrid change. The Word was made Man. It puts on flesh and blood and begins to give itself airs.

16

MARCH

· *15* ·

A curious sensation, to delve into one's own past; one is inclined at times to ask whether the record can be authentic.

· *16* ·

Ladies do not like being called icebergs. Such remarks are always rude, and often incorrect.

· *17* ·

Britons never shall be slaves. What else are we?

· *18* ·

Life is full of untapped sources of pleasure. Education should train us to discover and exploit them.

· *19* ·

Some of us are supposed to produce our best efforts under the stimulus of privations; such a state of affairs paralyses my initiative. I must be well fed, like those mousing cats who capture mice not to still the pangs of hunger but for sport.

· *20* ·

So it is, with the young. From them you may learn what their elders, having forgotten it, can nevermore teach you.

· *21* ·

How hard it is, sometimes, to trust the evidence of one's senses! How reluctantly the mind consents to reality!

· *22* ·

What is virtue? The conduct which conduces to the actor's welfare, the line of least resistance along which the sage walks and the fool is driven or kicked.

· *23* ·

It is not only Arabs who daze their understandings with godly ejaculations, oft repeated.

· *24* ·

All men fall into two main divisions: those who value human relationships, and those who value social or financial advancement. The first division are gentlemen; the second division are cads.

18

· *25* ·

Nothing like a solemn oath. People always think you mean it.

· *26* ·

How many things a race can do which its component members, taken separately, would blush to imitate!

· *27* ·

Somebody, one of these days, must be good enough to write a short sketch of the chief meddlers who have afflicted mankind, meddlers spiritual and also temporal—Julius Caesar, Napoleon . . .

· *28* ·

No one can aspire to be a philosopher who is in an incomplete state of physical development.

· *29* ·

You can live without friends, without wife or children or money or tobacco; you can live without a shirt, without a reputation; you cannot live without a document establishing your servitude to bureaucracy.

19

· *30* ·

We could not live without those whose business it is to bring the reasonableness of the few into its proper relief.

· *31* ·

What a pity that Latin, as scholars' language, for the definition and registration of ideas, was ever abandoned! There would be a cross-fertilization of cultures. As things now stand, half the intellectuals of this world are writing about matters which, unbeknown to themselves, have already been treated by the other half.

APRIL

· 1 ·

Duty has become the Moloch of modern life.

· 2 ·

No love-joy comes to bodies misfed, nor shall any progress in knowledge come from them.

· 3 ·

What is all wisdom save a collection of platitudes?

· 4 ·

They are all alike, these humanitarian lovers of First Causes. Always ready to burn something, or somebody; always ready with their cheerful Hell-fire and gnashing of teeth.

· 5 ·

That doctrine of elective affinity—what an ugly word for so lovely a thing!

· 6 ·

If we always knew from what motives our profoundest convictions have sprung!

· 7 ·

. . . our English church, whose *demi-vierge* concessions to common sense afford seductive resting-places to the intellectually weak-knee'd.

· 8 ·

It is always easy to discover defects in our favourites, once we have grown tired of them.

· 9 ·

Ever alert in his cage, my sallow siskin trills through the noonday hours, mindful of marvels he saw in dewy Sarmatian glades. For nothing escapes his eye. Ah, sprightly fowl, could mine enemy see what thou hast seen!

· *10* ·

Caste-feeling underlies every form of refine-
ment; it is a man's best prophylactic against that
mass-feeling which would make a cypher of him.

· *11* ·

There is as much grace and dignity in a European
existence just now as there is in a fat bourgeoise
running after an omnibus.

· *12* ·

Is there anything more charming than a
thoroughly defective verb?

· *13* ·

A retrospect of life is a chain, a broken chain,
of remembered moments.

· *14* ·

Mediaeval minds knew many truths, hostile to
one another. All truths are now seen to be inter-
dependent.

23

· *15* ·

The most dismal fact on earth, that brachycephalism is a Mendelian dominant.

· *16* ·

A subtle influence, no doubt, penetrates to the heart of man from the mere form and disposition of inanimate things.

· *17* ·

Nobody can misunderstand a boy like his own mother.

· *18* ·

The world is growing too narrow; congested and crammed with unpleasantness and deified "masses"; we gasp for fresh air.

· *19* ·

There is a beauty in mechanical fitness which no art can enhance.

· 20 ·

Our reverence for inspired idiots: has it never struck you?

· 21 ·

Nothing can be called beneficial in an ethical sense which does not commend itself as physiologically desirable.

· 22 ·

Some of us learn to make the best of a bad job. Few learn to make the best of a good one.

· 23 ·

Self-indulgence—it is what the ancients blithely called "indulging one's genius." How all the glad warmth and innocence have faded out of that phrase!

· 24 ·

The human heart has been constructed on somewhat ungenerous lines. Moralists may generalize with eloquence from the masses, but our poets have long ago succumbed to the pathos of single happenings.

25

· 25 ·

Deprived of chocolate, your lover of serving-maids is deprived of a persuasive helpmate.

· 26 ·

Far too many excellent people are rushing about needlessly, groaning under a load of duties to be performed and puzzling how to avoid them.

· 27 ·

Odd, how a uniform can fill a simpleton with self-importance.

· 28 ·

He was the worst kind of Englishman; he could not even cheat without being found out.

· 29 ·

This impatience or strenuousness is the white man's characteristic, and his curse.

· *30* ·

The boy of the streets, who sees nothing of the witchery of flowers and living waters, is not a veritable boy at any time, since his youth is ended ere it began.

MAY

· 1 ·

Pleasure—an end in itself, and the worthiest occupation for freeborn folk.

· 2 ·

There is a spell, a tawdry kind of spell, in these extramural regions; the outskirts of a town have more character than its centre.

· 3 ·

We must take a little account of the Cosmos nowadays; it helps to rectify our bearings.

· 4 ·

Coming events cast their shadows before. Phillida's coming baby will cast no shadow for several months.

· 5 ·

If we enlarge our concepts we should likewise enlarge our vocabulary.

· 6 ·

Questioning moods grow burdensome with years; after a strain of virile doubt we are glad to acquiesce once more. . . . The dog to his vomit.

· 7 ·

The ambiguous members of a man's family may not be the worst.

· 8 ·

Oral tradition alone can create demi-gods— hence their mysterious disappearance in these latter days of memoirs and newspapers.

· 9 ·

A man can believe a considerable deal of rubbish, and yet go about his daily work in a rational and cheerful manner.

· 10 ·

Whoever wants to save time is not fit for the society of gentlemen.

· 11 ·

The law does not content itself with classifying and punishing crime.   It invents crime.

· 12 ·

The families of one's friends are always a disappointment.

· 13 ·

Are we never to learn that Socialism has its roots in envy and in nothing else?

· 14 ·

Good intentions—no.   Nobody need attempt such an imposture on his stomach, an upright and uncompromising organ which refuses to listen to nonsense.   Or let them try the experiment. Gastritis will be the result of good intentions.

· *15* ·

We always talk of putting ourselves in our neighbours' places; idlest of phrases! since we cannot avoid bringing our personal apparatus to bear on their problems.

· *16* ·

Nobody must be protected against himself.

· *17* ·

Can anything be called a book unless it forces the reader by one method or another, by contrast or sympathy, to discover himself?

· *18* ·

To Hell with work. The man who talks to me about work is my enemy.

· *19* ·

Were a man to know what his fellow truly thinks; could he feel in his own body those impulses which drive the other to his idiomatic acts and words—what an insight he would gain!

MAY

· 20 ·

All sentimentalists are criminals.

· 21 ·

Love-visions are mirages at which no traveller has slaked his thirst.

· 22 ·

That passion for intervals of solitude—so natural and healthful to a boy, so incomprehensible to his teachers . . .

· 23 ·

Enlightened individuals crop up in the most unlikely places and epochs; enlightened groups of them are as rare as a flock of white blackbirds.

· 24 ·

The hours one wastes with these gods . . .

· *25* ·

Why bear a Cross?   Is it pleasant?   Is it pretty?

· *26* ·

Everything has shifted since *homo sapiens* himself shifted and ceased to be the hinge of the universe.

· *27* ·

The unseemly haste in rising! One might really think the company were ashamed of so natural and jovial a function as that to which a dining-room is consecrated.

· *28* ·

How often do the sensuous needs and pleasures of civilization coincide with those of wilder stages! There is a neo-barbarism not only in matters of art.   The sage—that perfect savage.

· *29* ·

To man it has been given to muse despairingly upon the progress of his own decrepitude, and contemplate at ease the workings of a calamitous contrivance whereby his person is transformed from fairness into a grotesque.

MAY

That peculiar College aroma which the most heroic efforts of a lifetime often fail to dissipate.

In my eyes the ever-changing Cosmos has lain serenely distended since pre-adolescent days, and by this time I am more than ever tired of Great Beings and their conjuring tricks. As to that other God, the source of earthly goodness—He is the protégé of vested interests. Abolish them, and He evaporates.

JUNE

· 1 ·

The villainies of the virtuous: who shall recount them?

· 2 ·

This starvation-fare may suit a saint and turn his thoughts heavenward. Mine it turns in the other direction.

· 3 ·

Why seek for reasons? They are so hard to find. One tracks them to their lair and lo! there is another lurking in the background, a reason for a reason.

· 4 ·

Man, the infatuated idealist, created, in one of his moments of mediaeval vapours, the Madonna-woman. . . . Whenever you catch yourself thinking that women are saints and angels, be sure you take a blue pill.

35

· 5 ·

That cenotaph! Let me devour mine, while daylight lingers, with some tender darling; then pitch me, after death, into what Acherusian swamp you please.

· 6 ·

There is so much goodness in real life. Do let us keep it out of our books.

· 7 ·

Let there be no virgins in the land!

· 8 ·

Man's field of enquiry used to be limited, while his credulity was unlimited. It is now the reverse in both cases.

· 9 ·

There are no false notes in Mohammedanism, no patches. It simplifies our existence, and scorns its calamities. Above all, you have the joy of finding yourself among real men. This religion has not sapped our self-respect.

36

· *10* ·

Our gods reflect the hearts that make them.

· *11* ·

In the usefulness of truth lies the hope of humanity.

· *12* ·

No race has yet been so rich that it could afford to exhibit the ideal of goodness which is frequently observed in the individual.

· *13* ·

It is the prerogative of vulgarians to be shocked.

· *14* ·

There exists in the languages both of Anglo-Saxons and of Teutons some elvish and industrious ferment which tends to produce a saccharine deposit . . . the mischief has its roots in our Gothic distrust of clean thinking.

· *15* ·

Love is ever love, to arouse whose fairest manifestations will call for varying demeanour.

· *16* ·

The apotheosis of the god-favoured loafer is drawing to a close.

· *17* ·

Rhetoric serves as a sign-post to true sentiment; it corresponds to some underlying state of mind and dare not express what is palpably incongruous or inept.

· *18* ·

Only think: a thousand wrongs to every right. What an opening for a man of talent. . . .

· *19* ·

How many avenues of delight are closed to the mere moralist or immoralist, who knows nothing of things extra-human, who remains absorbed in mankind and its half-dozen motives of conduct, so unstable and yet for ever the same. . . .

38

· *20* ·

There must be reasonable men everywhere; men who refuse to wear away their faculties in a degrading effort to plunder one another, men who are tired of hustle and strife.

· *21* ·

A Great Being who sets the Cosmos in motion and then goes to sleep: that will pass. One who remains awake and responsible for all that happens on Earth is a monster.

· *22* ·

Is it not the prerogative of civilized man to pause and ponder before the relics of his own past?

· *23* ·

The eye of youth dilates and distorts the images. The focussing process is painful. Youth has no norm.

· *24* ·

I wish the English still possessed a shred of the old sense of humour which Puritanism, and dyspepsia, and newspaper reading, and tea drinking have extinguished.

· *25* ·

The comfortable but preposterous fiction of the perfectibility of mankind.

· *26* ·

That iridescent charm of sexlessness which somebody, one of these days, must be good enough to analyse for us. . . .

· *27* ·

To be miserly towards your friends is not pretty; to be miserly towards yourself is contemptible.

· *28* ·

Can a man subscribe to the aspirations of a mob and yet think well of himself? Can he be black and white?

· *29* ·

We are rearing up a brood of crafty egoists, a generation whose earliest recollections are those of getting something for nothing from the State.

JUNE

We do get sadly out of perspective with our
environment in the fevered North, out of touch
with elemental and permanent things; we are for
ever looking up-stream.

JULY

· 1 ·

What you cannot find on earth is not worth seeking.

· 2 ·

All mankind is at the mercy of a handful of neurotics. Neurotics and their catchwords. . . . How we love tormenting ourselves!

· 3 ·

Christians are only an anaemic variety of Jews.

· 4 ·

That is the worst of dining with a man. You have to be civil next morning.

JULY

· 5 ·

Europe has lost her smile.

· 6 ·

I often wonder why men are so full of bitterness towards each other. It is one of those things I shall never live to understand.

· 7 ·

Learn to foster an ardent imagination; so shall you descry beauty which others pass unheeded.

· 8 ·

Good taste in viands has been painfully acquired; it is a sacred trust. Beware of gross feeders!

· 9 ·

The idealistic male with his cult of principles is the curse of Europe. He will die for his principles; no harm in that. He will persecute others for his principles, and this is what makes him such a nuisance.

· 10 ·

A supply of men who have not inhaled that poison-gas of education which paralyses our nerve-centres of independent thought would be a national asset in times of stress.

· 11 ·

Wherever there are enclosing walls, there are abuses behind them.

· 12 ·

Our social machinery is clogged by what were once adaptations and are now anachronisms as useless and menacing as the vermiform appendix.

· 13 ·

Heaven shield me from a clean-minded man!

· 14 ·

That is what the Press can do. It vitiates our mundane values. It enables a gang to fool the country.

· *15* ·

We live but once; we owe nothing to posterity; and a man's own happiness counts before that of anyone else.

· *16* ·

I can conceive the subtlest and profoundest sage desiring nothing better than to retain, ever undiminished, a childlike capacity for simple pleasures.

· *17* ·

Because she once dreamt of a shipwreck, our prudent Abbess has ever since declined to enter a bath.

· *18* ·

Your born lover bides entranced, caring little for the how and wherefore. He will close an eye, and see the better for it.

· *19* ·

The genii of earth and air were ready enough to commune with untutored men of early ages, to whom everything unknown was miraculous.

· 20 ·

Can our imagination ever create? Or must it not rather content itself with forming new combinations, with readjusting material that already lies at hand, if we care to pick it up?

· 21 ·

The present age, for all its cosmopolitan hustle, is curiously suburban in spirit.

· 22 ·

It is with Death as it is with God—we call them good because we are afraid of what they can do to us.

· 23 ·

Our sense of private dignity can survive the most oppressive man-despot; the despotism of law corrodes it.

· 24 ·

Take away from modern poetry what appeals to primitive man—the jingle and pathetic fallacy—and the residue, if any, would be better expressed in prose.

· 25 ·

Life in cheap and ugly homes cannot fail to give their inmates a corresponding bent of mind.

· 26 ·

Men who talk about the Dignity of Labour had better say as little as possible about civilization, for fear of confusing it with the North Pole.

· 27 ·

Leisure is the curse of the poor in spirit.

· 28 ·

Monogamous habits have been many a bard's undoing.

· 29 ·

One seldom presses books out, nowadays. . . . We browse dispersedly, in goatish fashion, instead of nibbling down to the root like that more con-scientious quadruped whose name, if I mentioned it, would degrade the metaphor.

47

· 30 ·

The most enlightened of legislators may well tremble to engraft the fruits of modern psychological research upon the tree of law, lest the scion prove too vigorous for the aged vegetable.

· 31 ·

I find everything useful and nothing indispensable. I find everything wonderful and nothing miraculous. I reverence the body. I avoid first causes like the plague.

AUGUST

· 1 ·

Incorruptibility is the fetich of the half-civilized.

· 2 ·

Man being master of his life—it will soon be the only thing he can call his own—suicide is his unalienable right.

· 3 ·

Be pleasant to everybody, and everybody will take you to be pleasant. And if you can be reasonable at the same time—why, so much the better.

· 4 ·

One would think that Commerce, which has broken down geographical barriers, would have done the same to political ones. Far from it! In sharpening men's lust for gold, it has demarcated our frontiers with a bitterness hitherto unknown.

AUGUST

A two-thousand years' course of "believing the impossible" cannot but debase the general standard of intelligence.

· 6 ·

The true cook is the perfect blend, the only perfect blend, of artist and philosopher. He knows his worth: he holds in his palm the happiness of mankind, the welfare of generations yet unborn.

· 7 ·

Nine-tenths of the reformers of humanity have been mischief-makers or humbugs.

· 8 ·

What joy to listen to analphabetics for a change: they are undubitably the Salt of the Earth.

· 9 ·

Cheese, a bad supplement for a meal but a good complement.

· *10* ·

To want a wife is better than to need one. Especially if it happens to be only your neighbour's.

· *11* ·

Over-government is killing self-respect, and hustle is killing ease of soul.

· *12* ·

I wonder how much they would have to pay me to be an English private-school boy again.

· *13* ·

Progress subordinates. Civilization co-ordinates. The individual emerges in civilization. He is submerged in progress.

· *14* ·

We find it a strain to sympathize with the griefs, however acute, however sincere, of those whose head controls their heart.

51

· *15* ·

Indigestion and love will not be yoked together.

· *16* ·

I have gained the conviction—firm-fixed, now, as the Polar Star—that the Hebrew is as good a man as the Christian.

· *17* ·

Whoever despises the investigation of secondary causes is a menace to his fellow-creatures.

· *18* ·

Morality is the property of the crowd. It bears an inscription that damns it for all purposes of art: *connu !*

· *19* ·

Machine ages have no use for an aesthetic sense.

· 20 ·

The civilized attitude! Your vulgarian cannot achieve this point of view. For all his effrontery he is a slave—a slave to his own poor soul, to a thousand prejudices and taboos.

· 21 ·

Man first appeases, then worships, his devils.

· 22 ·

Scientific curiosity and commercialism, parents of fair talk and fair dealing among men, retire discomfited when there are immortal souls to be saved.

· 23 ·

How many noble shapes acquired a tinge of absurdity in the Middle Ages!

· 24 ·

The school-age is continually being raised. Soon we shall be doing sums when we might be getting married.

· *25* ·

Shall evil be done that good may come of it; has anything ever been gained by denying a well-established fact?

· *26* ·

I glance down the ages and see nothing but— change! And perhaps not even change. Mere differences of opinion as to the value of this or that in different times and places.

· *27* ·

The arousing of desire is one thing; power to act is another, and such power is what your lover seeks.

· *28* ·

I see no reason why men should desire to live in a Golden Age of literature, save in so far as that millennium might coincide with a Golden Age of living.

· *29* ·

It is the test of beauty and vitality that a beholder refuses to acquiesce at first glance. There is a conflict to be undergone.

· *30* ·

How love for a man not her husband will sharpen a woman's wits!

· *31* ·

Confide not in your face, however comely; many a blear-eyed hunchback has better luck. Nor yet in gold; some poor ostler will slip in to enjoy his mistress while her knight serenades at the window.

SEPTEMBER

· 1 ·

Public opinion is a public nuisance.

· 2 ·

Can a man who lacks sympathy with erring humanity give us a convincing picture of it?

· 3 ·

Perhaps there are two truths: the truth of fact and that of suggestion.

· 4 ·

Whether consciously or not, we cannot but be influenced by the *colour-effects* of mere words, that arouse in us definite but undefinable moods of mind.

· 5 ·

A fellow can't live without vices.

· 6 ·

Envy makes strange bed-fellows.

· 7 ·

We have lost our bearings in the search after gladness, if gladness be what we are seeking. And what else should an intelligent man seek?

· 8 ·

Conscience is a good servant but a bad master.

· 9 ·

Is there some master-key to the problem of the differentiation of closely allied species? What peculiar trait caused the chiff-chaff, wood warbler, and willow warbler to diverge from the parent stock and from each other?

· 10 ·

You can construct the character of a man and his age not only from what he does and says, but from what he fails to say and do.

· 11 ·

He is the favourite of the Gods who knows the right word, and when to utter it.

· 12 ·

Burn your boats! This has ever been my system in times of stress.

· 13 ·

Home influence, as Grace Aguilar conceived it—where has it gone? . . . We are heading straight for the jaws of that obscene monster—the "Community."

· 14 ·

How one longs to engrave certain memories upon the brain, to keep them untarnished and carry them about on one's journeyings in all their freshness!

· 15 ·

Men, refusing to believe what is improbable, reserve their credulity for what is utterly impossible.

· 16 ·

Why always "not yet"? Do flowers in spring say "Not yet"?

· 17 ·

Acts sit tight, while social conditions change and our knowledge of man's nature moves forward; the discrepancy between law and reason is often acute.

· 18 ·

Metaphysicians are poets gone wrong.

· 19 ·

There is in most of us a lyric germ or nucleus which deserves respect; it bids a man ponder, or create; and in this dim corner of himself he can take refuge and find consolations which the society of his fellow-creatures does not provide.

59

· 20 ·

I always feel as if I needed a bath after talking about religion.

· 21 ·

Perhaps one should not think so much of oneself, though it is an interesting subject.

· 22 ·

A child is ready to embrace the universe. And, unlike adults, he is never afraid to face his own limitations.

· 23 ·

Fresh counsel is like fresh water—never to be swallowed with impunity.

· 24 ·

Have you not noticed that whenever anything, however fantastic, is imposed upon men by physical forces, they straightway make a god of it?

· *25* ·

Speaking for myself, I've had enough goodness for the present. It's worn me to a skeleton, I declare. . . .

· *26* ·

He was a curious delver, one that divined the worthiest and vainest pursuit of man, who concerned himself with the Elixir of Life.

· *27* ·

The cad is a product of education.

· *28* ·

Imperialism is an undiluted mischief, and all its offspring are mischief . . . that poisonous nationalistic spirit, the curse of humanity, the modern *infâme*.

· *29* ·

Life must be lived, not endured.

· 30 ·

The Church of England: what was it still good for? A stepping-stone, possibly, towards something more respectable and humane.

OCTOBER

· 1 ·

We have too much sex on the brain, and too little of it elsewhere.

· 2 ·

The image of the South is not seen so clearly on the spot as when it rises like an exhalation before the mind's eye amid hyperborean gloom.

· 3 ·

Mankind is curiously melodramatic; full of affected reverence for its droll little institutions.

· 4 ·

The newspaper and the crank, as custodians of public right and wrong, have begun to step into the shoes of the priest, with a little unnecessary noise.

· 5 ·

One can always trust to time. Insert a wedge of time, and nearly everything straightens itself out.

· 6 ·

I think knowledge should intensify our pleasures. That is its aim and object, so far as I am concerned.

· 7 ·

Distrust of authority should be the first civic duty.

· 8 ·

The philosopher can only live under a venal government.

· 9 ·

Cherish the living, whose hearts may yet be gladdened. There is no gladdening a corpse, try as we may.

· *10* ·

Men are becoming blind to these and other uglifications—the word is not quite ugly enough for the thing—of the scenery and of their houses.

· *11* ·

The only warfare worthy of the name is the bloodless crusade against fools.

· *12* ·

The mendicant friar, that flower of Oriental ethics—he is not up to date. He lacks self-respect. He apologizes for being alive. It is not pretty, to apologize for being alive.

· *13* ·

If I ever felt inclined to blush it would not be at the crooked behaviour of men, but at their crooked intellectual processes.

· *14* ·

Whenever people make fools of themselves, they always try to get God to pull them out of their scrapes. And, by Jove! sometimes they succeed.

OCTOBER

· 15 ·

Chastity is an insult to the Creator and an abomination to man and beast.

· 16 ·

A fasting stomach and a full one have nothing in common save this: both are enemies to love.

· 17 ·

Theology has left the Mark of the Beast upon our Statute-Book.

· 18 ·

He is no sound judge in any department of human endeavour who fails to identify himself with the creator's point of view, however repugnant it may be to his own.

· 19 ·

Thirty-nine. It is a good age. One begins to appreciate things at their true value.

· *20* ·

A certain young rogue at Phaleron begs in one breath for a toy steamboat and a real girl. Zeus dear, what shall I do about it?

· *21* ·

I always know when a man is drunk, even when I'm drunk myself.

· *22* ·

The ethics of modern state-craft: to what hairy anthropoid must we go back in order to find a justification for them?

· *23* ·

One would like to know how much of an Englishman's time and energy is consumed in trying to circumvent regulations which ought not to exist.

· *24* ·

That nameless protean evil, which refuses to see things as they are, sometimes takes the shape of patriotic emotionalism, and then produces an acute and contagious disorder that can nowise be tolerated in polite society.

· 25 ·

The ideal author of travel-books is the inspired, or at least enthusiastic, amateur.

· 26 ·

The poor in mind are like children in this, that they create realities to coincide with emotional states; and for such as these, they say, is the Kingdom of Heaven reserved.

· 27 ·

Renunciation has always exercised an irresistible attraction for good society.

· 28 ·

It is a wondrous voyage when one remounts the meanderings of that river Thought, which flows unceasingly, day and night, from birth to death. What dim, half-forgotten landscapes one traverses!

· 29 ·

Our faults and our virtues are distilled for us beforehand in the silent laboratory of the past.

· 30 ·

Would you be young? Then live with the young, and flee the old with their aches and pains, their fretfulness and valetudinarian makeshifts.

· 31 ·

No modern of any race, I fancy, can divest himself of the notion that one man is as good as another; in the eyes of God, they add—meaning in their own eyes. No Greek, no ancient of any race, I fancy, could have burdened himself with so preposterous a delusion.

NOVEMBER

· 1 ·

Justice is too good for some men, and not good enough for the rest.

· 2 ·

Life was no longer a hurdle in a steeplechase to be taken at a gallop; it was a tangle of beastly facts that stared you in the face and refused to get out of the way.

· 3 ·

We lack the light touch in spiritual matters.

· 4 ·

Beings wholly divine are inevitably endowed with qualities of good and evil identical with our own; they are mere caricatures of good and bad men. The profoundly divine therefore is, and ever has been, profoundly uninteresting.

70

· *5* ·

A writer who succeeds in satisfying everybody should have his blood-pressure tested. Something must be wrong with him.

· *6* ·

Hearts do not change so quickly; we only weave new garments in which to clothe hopes and fears that are for ever old.

· *7* ·

The tenacity of nonsense!

· *8* ·

The ideal citizen is not the ideal man.

· *9* ·

It seldoms pays to be rude. It never pays to be only half rude.

· 10 ·

Animals also have their sufferings, but they are not encouraged to tell us about them. Perhaps that is why God made them dumb.

· 11 ·

Love your neighbour as yourself. Now what has that gentleman done to deserve our love?

· 12 ·

Opportunities for self-expression, for unauthorized pleasure however innocuous, are growing rarer from day to day. Love of freedom has been clipped and pruned in all its ramifications.

· 13 ·

It is the merit of the Roman Church that she has left us some grains of common sense in regard to minor morals.

· 14 ·

Wine is a precarious aphrodisiac, and its fumes have blighted many a mating.

· 15 ·

If you want to see what children can do, you must stop giving them things.

· 16 ·

If they had the wit to see through their witless gods, they would know better than to tear the spirit away from that body which should be its guide and friend.

· 17 ·

. . . that "hopefulness" with which the present generation loves to delude itself, in defiance of the teaching of all history.

· 18 ·

Truth blends well with untruth.

· 19 ·

Here we sit, huddled together like cattle in a pen, each one duly labelled as to his potential worth to the community, and controlled by a herd of guardians so increasingly large that the shepherds will presently outnumber the sheep.

· 20 ·

The author who sets out to address a crowd defeats his own object; he eliminates the essence of good writing—frankness. You cannot be frank with men of low condition.

· 21 ·

How often could things be remedied by a word. How often is it left unspoken.

· 22 ·

What is life well lived but a blithe discarding of primordial husks, of those comfortable intangibilities that lurk about us, waiting for our weak moments?

· 23 ·

Everything is worth talking about.

· 24 ·

All town-bred persons, with the rarest exceptions, are incomplete in a certain small sense of that word. They show a gap which, unlike other gaps (deficient learning or manners), can never be filled up in later years.

74

· 25 ·

Our Statute-Book is growing into a sinister contrivance for the protection and conservation of fools.

· 26 ·

Generations came and went, cities rose and crumbled to dust, old mountains put on new faces; a search for that which should replace the vigour of youth proceeded without abatement.

· 27 ·

How one changes—how one looks at things with other eyes!

· 28 ·

Graft abstract principles of conduct upon human natures devoid of sympathy and you produce a sanctimonious fish, the coldest beast that ever infested the earth.

· 29 ·

What a relief, moreover, to be able to talk to a gentleman for a change!

· *30* ·

I do not call to mind any passages in the Bible commending the temperate philosophic life, though it would be strange if so large a miscellany did not contain a few sound reflections.

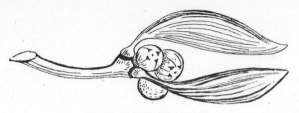

DECEMBER

· 1 ·

A lover who reasons is no lover.

· 2 ·

Every state of the mind, whether we are in society or alone, should be pressed to the last drop.

· 3 ·

To find a friend one must close one eye. To keep him—two.

· 4 ·

If one dream can be called more absurd than another, this of universal brotherhood is surely the absurdest that ever sat in our poor deluded brain, and the present state of the world a sound commentary on it.

F

DECEMBER

· 5 ·

Nothing ages a man like living always with the same woman.

· 6 ·

I have better uses for my leisure than to try to bring others round to any convictions of mine, such as they are.

· 7 ·

To tell you the truth, Nea-huni, I never shared your infatuation for mortals and their works.

· 8 ·

Give love to the young, who requite you with kisses; take no thought of *hic iacet*, which takes no thought of you.

· 9 ·

The Latin is either puerile or adult. The Englishman remains adolescent.

DECEMBER

· 10 ·

We can hardly realize, now, the blissful quietude of the pre-telephone epoch.

· 11 ·

By the aid of science millions of the best of our race are annihilated in a moment; by its aid millions of the worst are artificially kept alive, when they should be allowed to die.

· 12 ·

We are all lost sheep, and none the worse for that.

· 13 ·

Some trouble would have been avoided if Catholicism had never strayed beyond the Mediterranean basin. There, rooted in that old paganism—there is its home.

· 14 ·

A venerated Queen of Northern Isles reared to the memory of her loving Consort a monument whereat the nations stand aghast. Is this the reward of conjugal virtue? Ye husbands, be unfaithful!

DECEMBER

· 15 ·

The longer one lives, the more one realizes that nothing is a dish for every day.

· 16 ·

How good it is to be at home again, simmering and bubbling with contentment as you recognize the old things in their old places!

· 17 ·

It is the drawback of all sea-side places that half the landscape is unavailable for purposes of human locomotion, being covered by useless water.

· 18 ·

The pestilential theory, that life is given us on trust.

· 19 ·

The poet may be an inspired illiterate, the romance-writer an uninspired hack. They write well or badly, and there the matter ends. The historian who fails in his duty deceives the reader and wrongs the dead.

80

DECEMBER

· 20 ·

A man who reforms himself has contributed his full share towards the reformation of his neighbour.

· 21 ·

What is all this ferocious nonsense about strenuousness?

· 22 ·

The soul! That unhappy word has been the refuge of empty minds ever since the world began.

· 23 ·

The bowels of compassion: a wonderful old phrase. They ought to be kept open.

· 24 ·

A man is an in-dividual; he cannot be divided or taken to pieces; he cannot be expected to possess virtues incompatible with the rest of his mental equipment, however desirable such virtues may be.

81

DECEMBER

· 25 ·

Temperance? I should call it the exercise of our faculties and organs in such a manner as to combine the maximum of pleasure with the minimum of pain.

· 26 ·

The world has grown not only older since Pericles; it has grown stupider.

· 27 ·

We are apt to outgrow our teachers in wisdom, but whoever has helped us to a larger understanding is entitled to our gratitude for all time.

· 28 ·

The happiest life, seen in perspective, can hardly be better than a stringing together of odd little moments.

· 29 ·

You may cram a truth into an epigram; the truth, never.

· 30 ·

Knowledge is power, they say.   Knowledge is
not only power, it is good fun.

· 31 ·

Education creates a type instead of a character;
in other words, it instils uniformity, which is an
enemy of civilization.   It is a governmental contrivance for inculcating nationalism, another enemy
of civilization. . . . Something should be done about
our tragical education-fetich.

Printed in Great Britain
by T. and A. CONSTABLE LTD.
at the University Press
Edinburgh